JUL 2 2 1985 75¢
H10

D1733607

Text copyright © 1971 by
Julian May Dikty. Illustra-
tions copyright © 1971 by Rod
Ruth. International copyrights
reserved in all countries. No
part of this book may be re-
produced in any form, except
for reviews, without permission
in writing from the publisher.
Printed in the United States.
ISBN: 87191-078-0
Library of Congress Catalog Card Number: 78-156051

Cactus Fox

JULIAN MAY

Illustrated by Rod Ruth

Creative Educational Society, Inc., Mankato, Minnesota 56001

30515936

A male kit fox trotted through the desert night.
He was very tiny, about the size of a house cat,
with a tan coat and bushy tail. Behind him, his
mate and their three young waited for the food
he would bring.

Something rustled in the night-blooming cactus. The fox stopped, his huge ears listening. Two tiny elf owls, no bigger than sparrows, burst into the air. One caught a moth. The other, crying *wik-wik-wik-wik*, flew to its hole in a tall organ pipe cactus.

The kit fox moved on. Not even he could catch the swift elf owls. He prowled along the rim of a dry wash, which cut through the Arizona desert floor like a small canyon. The night was very hot. A dry wind blew through spiny mesquite trees.

The fox heard a scratching sound and he crouched
behind a barrel cactus. In a clearing near the
edge of the wash, four kangaroo rats were playing.
They bounded straight up into the air, twirling
and dancing on their long hind legs.

Kangaroo rats were the most important food for
the kit fox and his family. Here in the desert,
where water was often scarce, kit foxes obtained
both meat and drink by feeding upon the rats.
The rats themselves needed little water. Their
bodies were able to make water from the seeds
they ate.

The fox crept closer to the dancing rats, hunting them by smell and by sound. But before he could spring, a slender shape came rocketing out of the darkness. It was a sidewinder rattlesnake—a night hunter, like the fox—that tracked its prey by feeling the warmth of their bodies. As it seized one of the rats, the others fled into their holes.

The kit fox turned patiently away in search
of other food. He had a regular hunting
territory, which he circled nearly every night.
But tonight he found no more kangaroo rats, no
pocket mice, no packrats. Most of the small
plant-eaters were hiding from the hot wind.

The fox came to the edge of a highway and
paused. Two lights, gleaming like great eyes,
were coming. The fox walked into the middle
of the road and sat down, waiting. A green
pickup truck slowed down and stopped.

A park ranger leaned out of the truck and
shouted at the fox to get out of the way.
But the little animal only stared curiously.
Kit foxes do not fear man. Finally the
ranger honked his horn. This startled the
fox and he moved slowly to the side of the
road.

After the truck had driven on, the fox looked after its red tail-light. Then he began to trot along in pursuit. He went for several miles, not knowing he had come out of the park.

The wind blew stronger. In the northwest, orange lightning
lit the sky over the Growler Mountains. Far from home now,
the kit fox hurried toward twinkling lights ahead.

Unafraid, the fox trotted into a little town. It was different from any place he had ever been before. His huge ears picked up strange sounds—music, laughter, doors slamming.

A boy came out of a small adobe house and saw the fox sitting in a square of lamp-light. The animal sat back on his haunches and tilted his head. The boy laughed, spoke a few words, and went into the house. He returned with something in his hand and called to the fox.

It was a bone with a bit of meat on it. The fox came fearlessly to the boy, took the food, and carried it to the shadow of a tall saguaro cactus. There, gnawing and crunching, he made a small meal. The boy made friendly noises.

The fox waited hopefully, but the boy brought no more food. And the animal remembered his mate and the young foxes waiting. He moved off into the darkness to continue his hunt.

A new sound reached the fox's ears—strange
birds, clucking nervously because of the
lightning. He walked around a chicken coop,
trying to find a way inside. But the wire
netting was too tight.

Then a delicious smell came to him. He darted eagerly toward an open shed. There lay a large piece of meat. The owner of the chickens, long troubled by coyotes raiding his flock, had hidden a pellet of poison in the center of the meat.

The kit fox took the bait carefully in his mouth. There was
plenty here to feed his family. He began the long journey
home. There was no need to follow the road now. His instinct
led him straight across the open desert.

Lightning drew bright lines all across the sky. Thunder
began to crack and roll. A herd of javelinas, wild pigs of
the desert, raced across his path. They were heading for
shelter among the rocks.

The fox raced through the hot night, the poisoned meat
held tightly in his jaws. Miles away from him, a great
storm dumped its cargo of rain on the mountain slopes.
But no rain fell on the desert floor near the fox.

Now the fox entered a place where tumbled rocks made it hard to run. He turned aside, then went down into a dry wash. Its sandy bottom made a more comfortable footpath.

Suddenly the fox stopped. His large ears turned first this
way, then that. He felt a roaring sound that was deeper and
more lasting than the thunder. The ground beneath him shivered.

Still clutching the morsel of meat with its poisoned heart, the fox started to run. He scrambled for the bank of the dry wash, but it was too steep to climb. He darted to the other side and tried to get out of the canyon that way.

But before he could escape, a roaring flood
came down upon him. The waters of the mountain
storm, flowing over the ground instead of
sinking in, had poured into the once-dry wash
and turned it into a tumbling river.

The fox sank into the water. As he gasped for
breath, he felt the piece of meat slip away
into the torrent. The river carried him along,
sometimes above water, sometimes below. He was
nearly drowned when he felt his feet touch the
branches of an uprooted mesquite tree. Half-dead,
he pulled himself up above the water.

After a time the moon came out of the clouds.
The water level in the wash dropped quickly
and the flash flood was over. The fox crouched
in his tree as the warm wind dried his fur.
Finally, he made his way to safety.

Some animals had not been so lucky. The fox found a cottontail rabbit lying still on a rocky shelf below the bank. He took it.

Not far away, at the foot of a rocky hillside,
his family waited for him. The young foxes
rolled and played in the moonlight, waiting
patiently for the food their father would bring.

ABOUT KIT FOXES

The kit fox is the smallest fox in North America. Adults weigh about five pounds, less than a large cat. They can run very fast. Their large ears help them hear prey moving far away. Their food is mostly small rodents such as kangaroo rats, pocket mice, and ground squirrels. They will also eat quantities of grasshoppers.

Kit foxes mate for life. A den
with several entrances is dug
in soft soil, perhaps on a hillside, perhaps along a dry wash.
There the young are born in the
spring. At first the mother
nurses them while the father
brings her food. Later, the
young foxes learn to eat meat
brought to them by the parents.
They stay near the entrance to
the den until they are nearly
full-grown, playing about like
puppies.

The kit fox was once common in most of the desert Southwest and the southern Great Basin country between the Rockies and the Sierra. In many places it is in danger of disappearing today. It is poisoned by accident when it takes baits intended for coyotes. Hunters also shoot the little animal because it has so little fear of man.

Kit foxes can live safely in
national parks, monuments,
and wildlife preserves. This
story takes place in Organ
Pipe Cactus National Monument,
Arizona. This is one of the
places where kit foxes may be
seen, especially along the roads
at night.